American
JAZZ
LOUIS
ARMSTRONG

TAMRA ORR

Mitchell Lane
PUBLISHERS
P.O. Box 196
Hockessin, Delaware 19707

American JAZZ

Benny Goodman

Bessie Smith

Billie Holiday

Charlie Parker

Count Basie

Dizzy Gillespie

Louis Armstrong

Miles Davis

Ornette Coleman

Scott Joplin

PUBLISHER'S NOTE: The facts on which this book is based have been thoroughly researched. Documentation of such research can be found on page 44. While every possible effort has been made to ensure accuracy, the publisher will not assume liability for damages caused by inaccuracies in the data, and makes no warranty on the accuracy of the information contained herein.

AUTHOR'S NOTE: This story is retold using dialogue as an aid to readability. The dialogue is based on the author's research, which is detailed on page 44.

Printing   1   2   3   4   5   6   7   8   9

Library of Congress Cataloging-in-Publication Data
Orr, Tamra.
  Louis Armstrong / by Tamra Orr.
    pages ; cm. — (American jazz)
Includes bibliographical references and index.
ISBN 978-1-61228-264-0 (library bound)
1. Armstrong, Louis, 1901–1971—Juvenile literature. 2. Jazz musicians—United States—Biography—Juvenile literature. I. Title.
  ML3930.A75O77 2013
  781.65092—dc23
  [B]

2012008631

eBook ISBN: 9781612283401

PLB

Contents

A Night in Jail

Louis's eyes danced as he watched the mass of people surrounding him in the streets of Louisiana. It seemed as if everyone was laughing, shouting, and singing all at the same time. The beat of live music tumbled from clubs and restaurants. Flashes of colorful lights and booming explosions of overhead fireworks decorated the sky.

It was New Year's Eve 1913 in New Orleans, one of the wildest and most exciting cities in the country. Louis Daniel Armstrong and his friends were excited to be a part of the celebration. They had spent the last few hours singing on street corners for the pennies people threw their way. Now it was time to stop working and join the party.

Armstrong listened to the pop, pop, pop of the fireworks above him. Wait, what was that? He heard another sound mixed in with the explosions. What was it? He peered into the crowd. Here and there, a few people were shooting guns loaded with blanks. The popping sound added to the general noise of the night.

Twelve-year-old Armstrong thought of the perfect way to join in the fun. Without another thought, he ran through the streets he knew so well to the apartment where he lived with his mother, Mary Ann and his sister, Beatrice. He knew that his stepfather kept a .38 pistol in the house, and Louis wanted to find it.

He searched and searched. A few minutes later, he found it inside a trunk. Making sure that it was loaded only with blanks, he stuck the gun in his belt and ran to join his friends back out on the streets. Once he was in the middle of the crowd, Armstrong saw other kids he knew. They pulled a six-shooter out and shot blanks at him. "Get him, Dipper!" shouted his friends.[1] His wide smile had earned him the nickname of Dipper Mouth, or "Dipper" for short.

Laughing, Armstrong shot six blanks straight up into the air. It was perfect—just like he had imagined it would be. His friends laughed.

A nearby police officer did not find a young boy holding a gun and shooting it into the air—even one filled with blanks—funny at all. He reached out and grabbed Armstrong by the arms. " . . . all of a sudden two white arms hugged me, and I looked up and there was a big tall policeman," Armstrong recalled years later in an interview with *Life* magazine. "Boy, I thought the world was coming to an end."[2]

Instead of spending the rest of the night playing with his friends and welcoming in the New Year, Armstrong spent those long hours behind bars. He was scared and lonely and had no idea what was going to happen to him next. Would he go to prison? Would his mother be angry? What kind of trouble was he in? When would he get out?

Although he had a wonderful imagination, Armstrong could not possibly have pictured what would happen to him next. His night in jail channeled his life in a completely new direction. Up until then, he had struggled to keep enough food in his stomach, had worked long hours for very little pay, and had worried about helping his family. Those problems were about to end.

When morning came, Armstrong was taken to juvenile court. The judge's decision about his punishment changed the young boy's life. It also helped him to discover a passion that he had barely noticed before. New Year's 1913 was not only a new start for the world, but a brand-new start for Armstrong.

The city of New Orleans is known as the home of the biggest Mardi Gras celebration in the country. All year long, the city is the place to go to have fun, hear amazing music, and see incredible shows. The New Orleans of 1913 was not quite the same as it is now, but it was on its way to building this type of celebration reputation.

Located near the mouth of the Mississippi River, the city lured people from all types of places and backgrounds. Immigrants from many countries settled there, adding their traditions, languages, and styles of music to a growing mix of cultures.

Many of these people were blacks who were still adapting to their newfound freedom from slavery. Their music styles came with them and found a home in New Orleans. In this city, parades often filled the streets with energy and sound. Bands performed in parks, and music flowed from clubs, stores, restaurants, and homes. For musicians, New Orleans was like a banquet—with many flavors and tastes to try.

Mardi Gras

A Rough Start

Maryann "Mayann" Albert bent over to pick up the dirty linens and blankets off the floor. Work as a housekeeper was exhausting. She knew it did not help that she was pregnant. It made it harder to keep working when she was so tired, but she had no choice. She was only fifteen years old, and unmarried. She had met handsome William Armstrong, a factory worker, some months earlier, and now they were going to be parents. When she saw Willie again, she would tell him, but she knew the news would not please him either.

Mayann was right. Willie was too young and too busy to want to settle down and become a father. Their son, Louis Daniel Armstrong, was born on August 4, 1901 (although some records say it was July 4, 1900). Three weeks after the child was born, Willie left.

Louis's early years were difficult. His mother worked hard, but the family struggled to get all they needed to survive. For his first five years, the boy was raised mainly by his grandmother, Josephine. She washed clothes for a living.

Even after he went back to live with his mother, life was hard in Brick Row, which was a type of hotel. Louis never forgot the poverty of those days. He recalled digging through trash cans and dumpsters to find enough to eat. When his mother gave birth to a girl, she was named Beatrice, although quickly nicknamed Mama Lucy. With one more person in the family, it became even harder to survive.

First Job

When Louis was only six years old, he was already working. His first paying job was with a Russian family. The Karnofskys had two wagons. One was used to go through the city selling coal. The other one was used to buy and sell all kinds of things, from clothing to dishes. It was young Louis's job to call out to people and get their attention. "I was singing selling coal, 'Stone coal, lady! Nickel a water bucket!" he recalled to *Life* magazine.[1] Along with singing, he grabbed people's attention by playing a small tin horn the Karnofskys had given him. He seemed to have a talent for it.

One day while riding on the wagon, Louis spotted a little cornet in a store window. He was curious. Could he play songs on it? He wanted to find out, but the horn cost $5, more money than he had ever seen at one time. The Karnofskys loaned him the money, telling him he could work it off over time. In one of his autobiographical essays, Armstrong wrote, "That cornet was real dirty and had turned real black."[2] He polished it up, cleaned it out, and began to blow.

The Karnofskys encouraged him to keep learning. "As a Young Boy coming up," wrote Armstrong, "the people whom I worked for were very much concerned about my future in music. They could see that I had music in my Soul. They really wanted me to be something in my life. And music was it."[3]

Along with playing his new horn, Louis spent time singing and dancing on the street corners with three of his friends. "We was Little Mack, Big Nose Sidney, myself and Georgie Grey," he recalled. The quartet would go from place to place throughout the city to sing—and hope that people would pay them. "After we'd sung, we'd pass the hat," he said.[4]

A New Home

To make enough money to live, Louis quit school at age eleven. Only a year later, he found himself standing in juvenile court, waiting for the judge to sentence him for shooting the pistol at the New Year's Eve celebration.

The Armstrong family worked hard to make enough money to survive. Mary Ann Albert (center) depended on help from her family when William (left) left Louis and Beatrice (right) to her sole care.

The judge decided to send the young boy to the Colored Waif's Home for Boys. It was also referred to as the Municipal Boys' Home. Part of this school later became the Milne Boys' Home in 1933. Run by a black man named Captain Joseph Jones, the school was known for helping young people get a better start in life. When Louis arrived, it was mealtime. He was greeted with the sight of more food than he had ever seen. That was not enough to make him feel better, though. "I was so sad and homesick, I wouldn't eat for four days," he told *Life* magazine.[5]

Life inside the Waif's Home was very different for Louis. There was plenty of food, comfortable clothes, and warm blankets. The young people were taught a variety of skills, including cooking, cleaning, gardening, and carpentry. Best of all, the home had its own band.

Until then, Louis had only known how to play the tiny cornet and a slide whistle. He thought of himself mostly as a singer. When Peter Davis, the head of the band, asked Armstrong if he wanted to be a part of the band, the young boy was not sure how to respond. Finally he said yes, and Davis handed him a tambourine. "So I fool with that for a while," stated Armstrong in an interview, "then he give me a snare drum. . . . Then they give me an alto horn. . . . Then I got the bugle and just picked it up and started playing—blew reveille, mess call, taps every day."[6] When the home's lead cornet player left, Louis took his place. Soon he was the leader of the entire band. He had found his passion!

Louis stayed at the Waif's Home for more than a year and a half. At first he was released to live with his father, a man he had seldom seen while growing up. Soon, he was back with Mayann, Beatrice, and a new little boy, Clarence, the son of a cousin who had died in childbirth. Although he was still quite young, Louis did not return to school, a fact he always regretted. "But I had to take care of Mama . . . and at that time, I didn't need the schooling. I had the horn," he explained.[7]

The horn truly was Louis's ticket to the future. After years of struggling, he was about to find out that he had a musical gift that would not only surprise him, but astound and enchant much of the rest of the world.

The Karnofsky Project

The kindness and interest the Karnofsky family showed to Louis Armstrong lives on in the Karnofsky Project. The organization works to provide musical instruments and music lessons of all kinds to young people throughout New Orleans. Volunteers help encourage people in the community to donate instruments to children who could not otherwise afford them. More information can be found at http://www.karnofsky.org/.

Louis Armstrong playing trumpet with a young boy.

Chapter 3

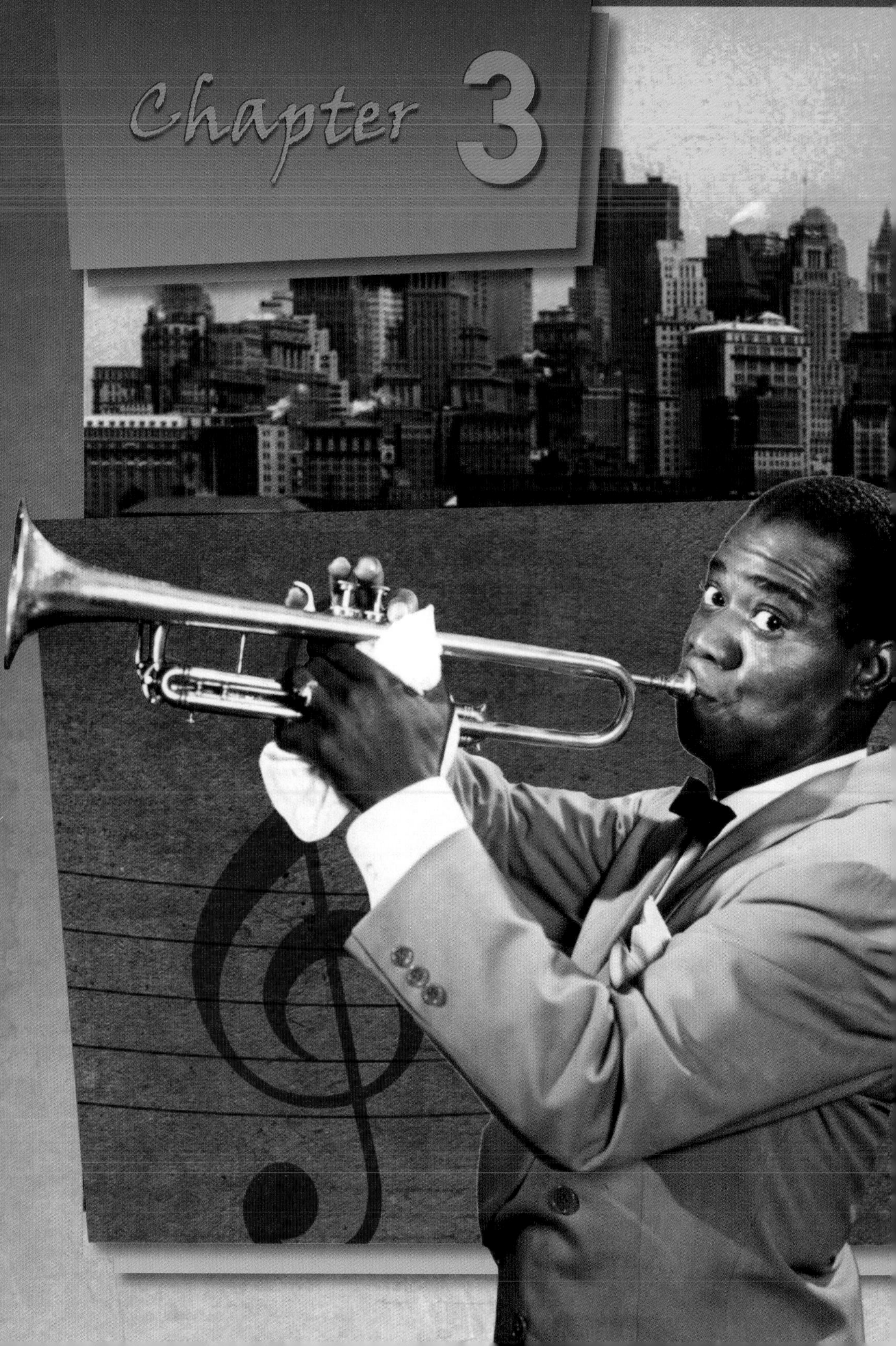

Finding
His Voice

Nothing made Armstrong happier than playing his cornet as the leader of the Colored Waifs' Home's band. He loved parading through the streets making music. Sometimes he would glimpse his mother watching him. She always looked so proud.

Finally, in the summer of 1914, it was time for him to leave the school. It was hard to say goodbye. He had learned a great deal there. "[The school] was the greatest thing that ever happened to me," Armstrong said in an interview. "Me and music got married at the home."[1]

For a brief time, he lived with his father, but soon, he was back with his mother and sister. He earned money selling newspapers and unloading banana boats, but he still managed to fit in time to listen to and play music.

An Important Friend

Not long after Armstrong returned home, he met Joe "King" Oliver, a man many considered one of the best trumpet players in New Orleans. Oliver took interest in this teen horn player, taking him under his wing to teach him musical tricks and talents. He even got him his first high-quality horn. Armstrong ran errands during the day, then shared the stage with Oliver and his Kid Ory band in nightclubs.

In 1918, when Oliver decided to move to Chicago, he asked Armstrong to take his place as the leader of the Kid Ory band. Armstrong said yes, and for the next few years he learned how to read music and play different styles of music.

Meanwhile, he met Daisy Palmer. Although their marriage did not last five years, his dedication to creating music did. He was playing for dancers and clubs, plus at funerals and parades. Not only did his skills on the horn get better and better, he also began trying new ways of playing. He became known for veering off the main notes of a song into a style called improvisation. This was a spontaneous series of notes that fit well with the main tune but changed from night to night. Armstrong was not the first musician to improvise when he played, but he was the one who made the technique popular. Today, almost all jazz musicians use improvisation in their performances.

Playing with Fate

Word of Armstrong's talent on the horn spread throughout New Orleans. Soon piano player and band leader Fate Marable hired the teenager to play on riverboats. These pleasure boats cruised up and down the Mississippi River from New Orleans to St. Louis. Some of these large steamboats carried as many as 5,000 passengers at a time. Armstrong played for three summers, and then Oliver invited him to join King Ory's band in Chicago. While he was there, he recorded his first of many albums. From Chicago, Armstrong went to New York to play with the Fletcher Henderson Orchestra. His fame was spreading.

It was here that he earned the nickname that spread around the world. Just as he had once been called Dippermouth for his big smile, now he was called Satchel Mouth, or Satchmo, for the same reason. When he performed, he made faces, smiled and talked to his audiences, told jokes, and rolled his eyes, all of which the crowd loved. In a magazine interview, Armstrong stated, "And all my little gestures, coming out all chesty, making faces, the jive with the audience clapping—aw, it's all in fun. People expect it of me; they know I'm there in the cause of happiness. What you're there for is to please the

King Oliver's Jazz Creole Band; (from left to right) Baby Dodds (drums), Honore Dutrey (trombone), Bill Johnson (bass), Louis Armstrong (second cornet), Johnny Dodds (clarinet), Lil Hardin-Armstrong (piano), King Oliver (cornet)

people—I mean the best way you can. Those few moments belong to them."[2]

The Art of Scatting

Before Armstrong became a horn player, he was a singer. As his popularity grew, he returned to singing, breaking into song in between verses on the trumpet. His unique voice was gravelly and rough, but in a way that charmed audiences. Along with improvising on his horn, Armstrong began using another free-form style in jazz music called

The happiness
Armstrong brought
to his audiences is
clearly reflected in
the joy that
performing brought
to him.

scatting. To scat, he would sing along with the music, but instead of using words or lyrics, he used nonsense words and syllables. This style of singing can be heard in one of Armstrong's most famous tunes, "Heebie Jeebies." Once again, he did not invent this style, but he helped make it known in every venue he played. It also inspired a number of other jazz performers to give it a try.

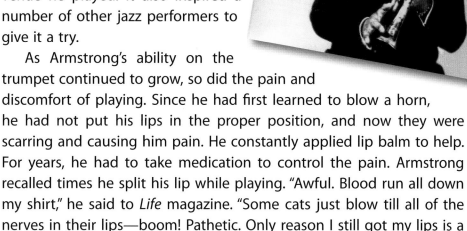

As Armstrong's ability on the trumpet continued to grow, so did the pain and discomfort of playing. Since he had first learned to blow a horn, he had not put his lips in the proper position, and now they were scarring and causing him pain. He constantly applied lip balm to help. For years, he had to take medication to control the pain. Armstrong recalled times he split his lip while playing. "Awful. Blood run all down my shirt," he said to *Life* magazine. "Some cats just blow till all of the nerves in their lips—boom! Pathetic. Only reason I still got my lips is a salve I keep; draws the tiredness out, keeps my lip strong."[3]

In 1924, Satchmo married again, this time to fellow band musician and piano player Lil Hardin. This marriage did not last long either, and the two divorced in 1931.

By this time, Armstrong was known throughout Chicago as "The World's Greatest Jazz Cornetist." He formed his own band called Louis Armstrong and his Hot Five, which later became The Hot Seven in 1927. Jazz fans throughout the country loved his style, and his star kept rising. He recorded almost two dozen albums, appeared on Broadway and in movies, plus acted as the headliner at countless jazz clubs. As much as he loved performing in cities like Chicago and New York, however, Armstrong was homesick for his hometown of New Orleans. It was time to go back where he started.

Louis Armstrong and his Hot Five was a popular jazz band throughout Chicago. Armstrong's wife, Lil Hardin, played piano and they kept the clubs hopping with dancing crowds.

Satchmo was so popular that just his name and smiling face on a poster was enough to bring in the fans.

The Horn Player's Embouchure

As any musician knows, how you hold and use the instrument controls what kind of sound you get from it. If you hold it too tightly, it can muffle the sound. If you press keys too hard, it will change the tone of the music. For horn players, the control of the sound depends on the musician's embouchure, a French word that means "to flow into the mouth." It refers to the position and use of the lips, tongue, and teeth when playing an instrument like a horn. If the position is not done properly, not only will the notes not sound as you want them to, but you can injure yourself. Armstrong learned how to play the horn by himself and was never taught correct embouchure. Although he managed to create some of the world's best jazz music, he also did severe damage to his lips and mouth.

Although Armstrong's style was unorthodox, his music was wildly popular.

Rising Star

When Armstrong returned New Orleans in June 1931, he was astonished by the welcome he received. More than half a dozen jazz bands were playing in his honor. Hundreds of people had lined up to catch a glimpse of him. He was carried on the shoulders of fans and was amazed to see that stores and even the local baseball team had been named after him. In New Orleans, Louis Daniel Armstrong was a hero!

Despite his talent, his fans, and his fame, however, Armstrong still had problems. His original manager, Johnny Collins, had not done a good job in many ways. He overbooked Armstrong, forcing the musician to perform too many shows with too little time to rest and recover in between. Collins also failed to do proper accounting, and soon Armstrong ran into trouble because of money he owed to the Internal Revenue Service and others. In 1935, Armstrong found another manager, Joe Glaser, who did a much better job organizing the jazz player's career. Glaser remained his manager for the next 30-plus years.

Armstrong and his band still had to deal with the same problem that many African Americans had during this period of history: racial prejudice. The clubs where they played had all-white audiences because blacks were usually not allowed inside. If they were, they had to stand in the back. There were times when announcers refused to introduce Armstrong and his band because the musicians were black. When the band toured in other cities, they were sometimes forced to sleep in

Louis Armstrong (front row center, with legs crossed) and his band pose with members of the Colored Waif's Home Brass Band (later named the Municipal Boys' Home Brass Band) and their teacher (third row, right, bow tie), Peter Davis. As a child, Armstrong was a resident at the home and Davis one of his earliest music teachers.

their cars or on buses because hotels would not let them rent rooms. Restaurants would not serve them. In some places, Armstrong and his band were the first African Americans to be allowed to perform in that venue.

Finally, Armstrong and his band went to Europe to tour and perform in places such as England, France, Denmark, and the Netherlands. Racial prejudice was far less rampant there, and thousands of people came to hear Satchmo play.

Back to the States

In 1935, Armstrong returned to the United States. Some of his concerts were nationally broadcast over the radio, so people all over the country could enjoy listening to him play some of his biggest hits, such as

"When It's Sleepytime Down South," "Memories of You," and the amazing "Swing that Music," which features Armstrong hitting 42 high C's (difficult notes on the cornet) followed by a high E-flat.

In 1938, less than two weeks after his divorce from Lil Hardin became final, Armstrong married his third wife, Alpha Smith. Like his earlier marriages, however, this one did not last. The two divorced in late 1942. Shortly after, Armstrong finally found the love he was looking for when he married Lucille Wilson, the woman he would stay with for the rest of his life.

Armstrong's fame kept spreading as he not only performed on stage, but hosted the Fleischmann's Yeast Show radio program and appeared in movies such as *Going Places*, *Dr. Rhythm*, and *Cabin in the Sky*. He even provided his voice and trumpet-playing to a Betty Boop cartoon called "You Rascal, You."

A Home of his Own

Up until this point, Armstrong had lived in hotels and motels, moving from place to place to perform. In 1943, however, Lucille surprised her husband by buying a house in Corona, a part of Queens, New York. After a late performance, the jazz man took a cab to the new address Lucy had given him. In one of his essays, titled "Early Years with Lucille," he recalls the moment he saw his home for the first time. "So the cab driver finally found the house," he wrote. "And he . . . said to me, 'O.K., this is the place.' One look at that big fine house, and right away I said to the driver, 'Aw man, quit kidding!' "[1]

Armstrong was thrilled with it, and the couple lived there together for the rest of their lives. Years after buying the house, Armstrong told a magazine interviewer, "Ain't never going to move. My wife Lucille grew up here. I've watched every kid on the block grow up."[2]

As time passed, Satchmo and other jazz musicians had to learn new styles and songs to keep up with the changes around them. A few years after World War II ended in 1945, jazz began to lose popularity. Rock and roll music was the new fad. It introduced such stars as Elvis Presley and Jerry Lee Lewis, plus African American powerhouses such

During a visit to Gaza, Louis played the trumpet while his wife, Lucille, listened.

as Little Richard and Fats Domino. Armstrong realized that he needed to update his music style if he was to compete with musicians like these, so he began blending jazz with the familiar Big Band sound. He called his new band the Louis Armstrong All-Stars, and for the first time, the band combined black and white musicians. They performed a kind of jazz known as Dixieland.

Throughout the 1950s, Armstrong kept performing and touring, seeing countries as far away as Scandinavia, Australia, and North Africa. Although he was well known for his big smile, he was not smiling in 1957. The U.S. State Department sponsored a tour to the Soviet Union. He canceled the show to protest a racial injustice at home. Schools in Little Rock, Arkansas, refused to allow African American students into their classrooms. Benny Goodman, a Caucasian jazz man, was sent on the tour in Armstrong's place.

As the 1950s came to an end, Armstrong was at the top of the music charts. He was loved by countless fans all over the world. All of his hard work, travel, and dedication was taking its toll. While in Spoleto, Italy, to film a performance for *The Ed Sullivan Show* in 1959, Armstrong had a heart attack. Was it time to slow down?

Giving Back

Armstrong never forgot what it felt like to be poor and hungry. He did what he could to give back to his community. When he went out in public, he would carry two money rolls with him. One was for his use; the other was used to hand out to anyone who needed some spare change. During one concert he gave, Satchmo found out that many of the people in the area could not afford coal to heat their homes. Before the concert was over, everyone who attended was given a load of coal to take home. Armstrong once stated, "If I ever get poor, I'll still be happy. Like I always say, it's better to be 'once was' than 'never was.' "[3]

Seeing the World

The young boy singing on the street corner of New Orleans most likely never imagined that one day he would travel around the world to perform in front of thousands of adoring fans. However, that is exactly what Armstrong did throughout the 1960s. Despite growing health problems, Armstrong was determined to make his fans happy, no matter how far away they lived. He worked on improving his diet and losing weight, but he simply could not slow down his music.

As the decade began, Satchmo spent four months touring in multiple countries throughout Africa, including Ghana, Cameroon, Kenya, Nigeria, Sierra Leone, and Egypt. Between shows, he found time to write two autobiographies. He was often called "Ambassador Armstrong" for all the goodwill and happiness he spread when he visited foreign lands. At one concert in Ghana, more than 100,000 people showed up to hear him blow his horn. The African people called him Okuka Lokole (oh-KOO-kah luh-KOH-lay), which means "one who charms beasts with music."[1] He recorded a number of albums, and on May 23, 1963, he performed in a birthday celebration for U.S. President John F. Kennedy.

In 1964, the producers of an upcoming Broadway show called *The Matchmaker* asked Armstrong if he would be willing to record a song for the musical. They were hoping that his name would create public interest in the show. Armstrong agreed—and created one of his biggest hits of all time. The production's title was changed to *Hello, Dolly!* after the theme song, which was performed by Satchmo. The song was so popular that it even knocked the Beatles out of the number one position on the music charts. Decades later, it remained one of the two songs that most people think of when they hear the name Louis Armstrong.

Because *Hello, Dolly!* was such a huge hit, Armstrong was more in demand for talk shows, including *The Mike Douglas Show*, *The Dean Martin Show*, and *The Tonight Show*. He performed in Las Vegas, toured

Singing the theme song to *Hello, Dolly!* helped catapult Satchmo to stardom. Armstrong appeared in the film with actress Barbra Streisand.

Louis and Grace Kelly
on the set of the film
High Society in 1956

Eastern Europe, and appeared in more movies, such as *When the Boys Meet the Girls* and *A Man Called Adam*. His face was on the cover of magazines, including mainstream publications *Time* and *Life*. Soon, everyone knew who this jazz man was.

A Wonderful World

In 1967, Armstrong recorded another song that would one day be considered his signature song. "What a Wonderful World" was written to bring people hope. It climbed the charts a second time in 1987 when it was used on the sound track for the movie *Good Morning, Vietnam*. He also recorded a unique album of Disney movie songs, called *Disney Songs the Satchmo Way*, in 1968.

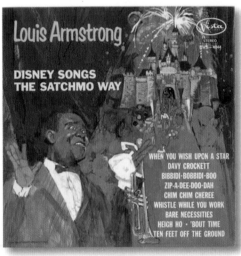

Throughout 1968 and 1969, Armstrong's demanding schedule caught up with him once again. He was hospitalized with heart and kidney problems a number of times. In between stays at Beth Israel Hospital, he continued to give concerts, even though his doctors advised against it. When his manager and close friend Joe Glaser died, Armstrong was devastated. Although his passion and talent were still strong, his body was wearing down, and as the new decade approached, he spent more and more time in the hospital.

In an essay he wrote for the December 1969 issue of *Esquire* magazine, Armstrong wrote about getting older. "My belief and satisfaction is that, as long as a person breathes, they still have a chance to exercise the talents they were born with," he stated. "And at the age of sixty-nine I really don't feel that I am on my way out at all. Of course a person may do a little less—but the foundation will always be there."[2] Unfortunately, the end was closer than Armstrong knew or was willing to admit.

The Silver Screen

Armstrong appeared in many different television shows and movies throughout his life. Like other African American actors of this time period, he faced the problem of racism, so he was limited to walk-on roles that could easily be deleted for some audiences. During his life, Armstrong appeared in:

A Rhapsody in Black and Blue (1932)
Cabin in the Sky (1943)
New Orleans (1947)
The Glenn Miller Story (1953)
High Society (1956)
Paris Blues (1961)
Hello, Dolly! (1969)

Armstrong played a band leader in, "The Lord Don't Play Favorites," on the television program Producers' Showcase in 1956.

Chapter 6

A Jazz Legend

Ignoring his doctor's advice to stop performing and start resting, Armstrong just kept playing. It was that important to him to please people and entertain audiences. In March 1971, he signed up to play for two weeks at New York's famous Waldorf Astoria Hotel. He spent the days in a hotel room resting, and then came downstairs each night to start blowing his horn in the hotel's Empire Room. His fans all noticed that he seemed weak, and indeed, the great Satchmo was slowing down, due to a combination of kidney, liver, and heart problems. He told fans, "I'm going back to work when my treaders [legs] get in as good shape as my chops [lips]." The performances he gave at the Waldorf were his last.

Only a day after his seventy-first birthday, Armstrong had a second heart attack. This time, he did not recover. The entire world mourned his loss. U.S. President Richard Nixon and his wife, Pat, released a statement to the press: "One of the architects of an American art form, a free and individual spirit, and an artist of worldwide fame—his great talents and magnificent spirit added richness and pleasure to all our lives."

At Armstrong's funeral, more than 25,000 people came to pay their respects. Outside the Corona Congregational Church in Queens, thousands more fans stood on the streets. Pallbearers, the people who carry the coffin to the cemetery, included famous jazz performers Dizzy Gillespie, Duke Ellington, Ella Fitzgerald, and Count Basie, as well as television celebrities Ed Sullivan, Johnny Carson, and Merv Griffin. One element that was missing from Armstrong's funeral was music. It was his request that no jazz be played. However, that silence ended the next day in the streets of New Orleans, where jazz bands paraded through the city playing to honor one of their own.

Armstrong left behind his wife, Lucille, of twenty-nine years. Although he never had any children of his own, he adopted his cousin Clarence, a young boy who was mentally impaired due to a severe fall when he was very young. Armstrong sometimes referred to the boy as "Little Louis Armstrong" and made sure he was taken care of all of his life.

The memory of Satchmo's great smile, incredible talent, and passion for the horn still lives on in jazz music today.

Handcolored etching and Photogravure
Satchmo (Louis Armstrong) by Adi Holzer, 2002

Continued Honors

The contribution that Armstrong made to both jazz music and American history is amazing. He changed how horns were played, how words were sung, how bands performed, and how African Americans were accepted into society. As jazz great Dizzy Gillespie said, "Louis Armstrong's station in the history of jazz is unimpeachable. If it weren't for him, there wouldn't be any of us." Another jazz star, Duke Ellington, agreed. He stated, "If anybody was Mr. Jazz, it was Louis Armstrong. He was the epitome of jazz and always will be. He is what I call an American standard, an American original."

In 1995, to honor Satchmo, the U.S. Postal Service issued a first-class postage stamp with his smiling face playing his horn. In 2001, a century after Satchmo was born, New Orleans named its international airport after him. A number of parks, schools, and other organizations also carry his name.

After Lucille's death in 1983, the Armstrong house in Corona, New York, was left to the New York City Department of Cultural Affairs. It later became a museum showcasing collections of his music, writings, and belongings. Since no other people have lived in the house, it is still full of the Armstrongs' furnishings and decorations. Guided tours are offered to visitors, including through the Japanese-style gardens outside the home.

Louis Armstrong may have had a challenging beginning in life, but he was able to accomplish amazing things. His songs are still enjoyed by millions of fans. The happiness and joy he has brought to people around the world will live on for years to come.

Pleasing the People

Time magazine cover, 1949

Countless people enjoyed listening to the musical gifts of Satchmo. As one journalist described him, "he was also known to have delighted millions around the world for his ebulliently sandpapery voice, his merry mangling of the English language and his great wide grand-piano keyboard of a smile."[4] It was always his goal to make people happy. He once stated, "I never tried to prove nothing, just always wanted to give a good show. My life has been my music, it's always come first, but the music ain't worth nothing if you can't lay it on the public. The main thing is to live for that audience, 'cause what you're there for is to please the people."[5]

Chapter 1   A Night in Jail
1. Louis Armstrong, *Satchmo: My Life in New Orleans* (De Capo Press, 1986), p. 34.
2. Richard Meryman, "An Interview with Louis Armstrong, An Authentic American Genius," *Life*, April 15, 1966, p. 99.

Chapter 2   A Rough Start
1. Richard Meryman, "An Interview with Louis Armstrong, An Authentic American Genius," *Life*, April 15, 1966, p. 99.
2. Louis Armstrong, *Louis Armstrong, In His Own Words* (New York: Oxford University Press, 1999), p. 15.
3. Louis Armstrong, *Satchmo: My Life in New Orleans* (De Capo Press, 1986), p. 39.
4. Ibid.
5. Richard Meryman, "An Interview with Louis Armstrong, An Authentic American Genius," *Life*, April 15, 1966, p. 101.
6. Ibid, p. 105.
7. Ibid, p. 106.

Chapter 3   Finding His Voice
1. Louis Armstrong: The Epitome of Jazz, http://www.southernmusic.net/louisarmstrong.htm
2. Richard Meryman, "An Interview with Louis Armstrong, An Authentic American Genius," *Life*, April 15, 1966, p. 116.
3. Ibid, p. 109.

Chapter 4   Rising Star
1. Louis Armstrong, *Louis Armstrong, In His Own Words* (New York: Oxford University Press, 1999), p. 15.
2. Richard Meryman, "An Interview with Louis Armstrong, An Authentic American Genius," *Life*, April 15, 1966, p. 100.
3. Ibid.

Chapter 5   Seeing the World

1. "Untitled Article," *Jet*, November 17, 1960, p. 57.
2. Louis Armstrong, *Louis Armstrong, In His Own Words* (New York: Oxford University Press, 1999), p. 15.

Chapter 6   A Jazz Legend

1. Albin Krebs, "Louis Armstrong, Jazz Trumpeter and Singer, Dies," *The New York Times*, July 7, 1971.
2. "Untitled Article," *Jet*, November 17, 1960, p. 57.
3. Louis Armstrong: A Cultural Legacy, http://www.npg.si.edu/exh/armstrong/
4. Albin Krebs, "Louis Armstrong, Jazz Trumpeter and Singer, Dies," *The New York Times*, July 7, 1971.
5. Louis "Satchmo" Armstrong, http://www.u-s-history.com/pages/h3768.html

1901 Louis Daniel Armstrong is born in New Orleans, Louisiana, on August 4, 1901. (Some records give his birth date as July 4, 1900.)

1907 He sings on street corners with other children; he works for the Karnofskys, who help him buy his first cornet.

1912 On December 31, he is arrested for shooting gun at a New Year's Eve celebration.

1913 He is sent to the Colored Waif's Home for Boys and discovers a passion for playing music.

1918 Louis marries Daisy Palmer; he plays with Fate Marable on steamboats.

1922 He moves to Chicago and plays with King Oliver's band.

1924 He marries Lil Hardin; moves to New York City to play with Fletcher Henderson.

1925 He moves back to Chicago and forms the Hot Five.

1927 The Hot Five becomes The Hot Seven.

1932 Louis travels to Europe and tours Britain for three months.

1933 Milne Boys' Home built from parts of the Colored Waif's Home for Boys.

1935 He hires Joe Glaser to be his manager.

1936 Armstrong writes his autobiography, *Swing That Music*.

1938 He marries Alpha Smith.

1942 He marries Lucille Wilson.

1943 They move to a house in Queens, New York.

1947 He forms the Louis Armstrong All-Stars.

1954 His book *Satchmo: My Life in New Orleans* is published.

1957 He speaks out against racial discrimination in Little Rock, Arkansas.

1959 Armstrong has his first heart attack.

1964 His song "Hello, Dolly" knocks the Beatles out of the #1 Billboard position—after they'd held that spot for three songs in a row.

1971 After another heart attack, Armstrong dies on July 6.

"Ain't Misbehavin' "
"Basin Street Blues"
"Black and Blue"
"Blue Yodel No. 9" with Jimmie Rodgers
"Copenhagen" (with Fletcher Henderson)
"Dippermouth Blues"
"Dream a Little Dream of Me"
"Heebie Jeebies"
"Hello, Dolly"
"High Society"
"I Can't Give You Anything But Love"
"I Get a Kick Out of You"
"I've Got the World on a String"
"Laughin' Louie"
"A Kiss to Build a Dream On"
"Let's Fall in Love"
"Mack the Knife" (with the All Stars)
"Mahogany Hall Stomp"
"Makin' Whoopie"
"Memories of You"
"Potato Head Blues" (with the Hot Seven)
"Rockin' Chair" (with Jack Teagarden)
"St. Louis Blues"
"Sleepytime Down South"
"Star Dust" (with his big band)
"Stompin' at the Savoy"
(with Ella Fitzgerald)
"Swing that Music"
"That Old Feeling"
"What a Wonderful World"
"When It's Sleepytime Down South"
"Wild Man Blues"
"You Can't Lose a Broken Heart"
(with Billie Holiday)
"You Rascal, You"

LOUIS ARMSTRONG

BOOKS

Armstrong, Louis. *Satchmo: My Life in New Orleans*. De Capo Press, 1954.

Elish, Dan. *Louis Armstrong and the Jazz Age*. New York: Children's Press, 2008.

Josephson, Judith Pinkerton. *Louis Armstrong*. Minneapolis, MN: Lerner Books, 2008.

Partridge, Kenneth. *Louis Armstrong*. New York: Chelsea House, 2011.

Raum, Elizabeth. *Louis Armstrong: Jazz Legend*. Mankato, MN: Capstone Press, 2007.

Shuman, Michael A. *Louis Armstrong: Jazz Is Played from the Heart*. Berkeley Heights, NJ: Enslow, 2007.

WORKS CONSULTED

Armstrong, Louis. *Louis Armstrong, In His Own Words*. New York: Oxford University Press, 1999.

Collier, James Lincoln. *Louis Armstrong: An American Genius*. New York: Oxford University Press, 1985.

Giddins, Gary. *Satchmo: The Genius of Louis Armstrong*. New York : De Capo Press, 2001.

Krebs, Albin. "Louis Armstrong, Jazz Trumpeter and Singer, Dies." *The New York Times*, July 7, 1971. http://www.nytimes.com/books/97/08/03/reviews/armstrong-obit.html

Meryman, Richard. "An Interview with Louis Armstrong, An Authentic American Genius." *Life*, April 15, 1966, p. 94. http://books.google.com/books?id=-VUEAAAAMBAJ&pg=PA94&lpg=PA94&dq=Louis+Armstrong+interview+Life+magazine+1966s&source=bl&ots=mgynyjyGzM&sig=H450UnS834VFBaPz_ysSMnpnVXg&hl=en&ei=lES4TceLOl76sAOdoZSpAQ&sa=X&oi=book_result&ct=result&resnum=3&ved=0CCQQ6AEwAg#v=onepage&q&f=false

Stricklin, David. *Louis Armstrong: The Soundtrack of the American Experience*. Lanham, Maryland: Ivan R. Dee, Publisher, 2010.

Teachout, Terry. *Pops: A Life of Louis Armstrong*. New York: Houghton Mifflin Harcourt Publishing, 2009.

"Untitled Article." *Jet*, November 17, 1960, p. 57.

"Untitled Article." *Jet*, July 22, 1971, p. 57.

ON THE INTERNET

Jazz Biographies: Louis Armstrong
    http://www.pbs.org/jazz/biography/artist_id_armstrong_louis.htm
The Karnofsky Project
    http://www.karnofsky.org/
Louis Armstrong: A Cultural Legacy
    http://www.npg.si.edu/exh/armstrong/
Louis Armstrong House Museum
    http://www.louisarmstronghouse.org
Louis "Satchmo" Armstrong
    http://www.u-s-history.com/pages/h3768.html
Louis Armstrong: The Epitome of Jazz
    http://www.southernmusic.net/louisarmstrong.htm
PBS Kids, Jazz Greats: Louis Armstrong
    http://pbskids.org/jazz/nowthen/louis.html

PHOTO CREDITS: Cover—Joe Rasemas; p. 4—Michael Ochs Archives/Getty Images; p. 7—Chris Graythen/Getty Images; p. II—Frank Diggs Collection/Getty Images; p. Bentley Archive/Popperfoto/Getty Images; pp. I7, I8, 20, 22, 3I, 33, 4I—cc-by-sa; pp. 2I, 28, 3I, 36, 43—Library of Congress; p. 24—Transcendental Graphics/Getty Images; p. 26—Bettman/Corbis/AP Images; p. 27—March of Dimes; p. 30—Hulton Archive/Getty Images; p. 37—Adi Holzer; p. 39—*Time*. Every effort has been made to locate all copyright holders of material used in this book. If any errors or omissions have occurred, corrections will be made in future editions of the book.

alto (AL-toh)—A singer or musical instrument with a lower, deeper tone.

big band—A jazz or dance band that is the same size as an orchestra.

cornet (kor-NET)—A valved musical instrument from the trumpet family.

creole (kree-OHL)—A person born in Louisiana but of French ancestry.

Dixieland (DIKS-ee-land)—A style of jazz originating in New Orleans with a strong four part rhythm played by a small group with horns and percussion.

ebulliently (eh-BYOO-lent-lee)—With great excitement or enthusiasm.

embouchure (om-BUH-shur)—The way the lips and mouth are positioned to play a musical instrument.

epitome (eh-PIH-tum-ee)—A person or thing that represents an entire concept or trait.

improvisation (im-prov-ih-ZAY-shun)—To make something up on the spot, nothing practiced or prepared, completely spontaneous.

Mardi Gras (MAR-dee GRAH)—An annual holiday in New Orleans that features parties, parades and a great deal of jazz music.

quartet (KWAR-tet)—A musical group made up of four people.

rhapsody (RAP-suh-dee)—An instrumental composition irregular in form and often improvised.

reveille (REH-vuh-lee)—A signal of a drum or bugle that is sounded early in the morning to wake people.

scat (SKAT)—To sing by making full or partial use of words or nonsense syllables.

waif (WAYF)—A young person who has no home or family.

Index

About the Author

Tamra Orr is the author of more than 250 nonfiction books for readers of all ages, including biographies of celebrities and sports stars. She graduated from Ball State University in Muncie, Indiana. She lives in the Pacific Northwest with her family. "What a Wonderful World" has been a special song to Orr all her life, and her appreciation of the song and the man who sang it has increased as she learned more about Satchmo and his dedication to music and joy.

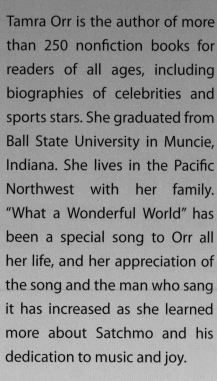